Infant Communion— Then and Now

by

David Holeton

Lecturer in Liturgy, Trinity College, Toronto
Member of the Doctrine and Worship Committee, Anglican Church of Canada

GROVE BOOKS

BRAMCOTE   NOTTS.

CONTENTS

ACKNOWLEDGMENT

This Study was originally given in substance as the annual Alcuin Club Lecture in October 1980, and its publication in this form is due to the kind permission of the Alcuin Club Committee.

THE COVER PICTURE

portrays the giving of communion to a young child in Nashotah House, a Theological seminary in the Episcopal Church of the United States of America, and is supplied by the Rev. Louis Weil who is portrayed in the picture.

First Impression September 1981

ISSN 0306 0608

ISBN 0 907536 09 3

INTRODUCTION

If, ten or fifteen years ago, one saw a notice for a paper on infant communion one could quite rightly expect a paper that dealt with the past and the East. Today that is no longer the case. In the past decade the question of communion for the very young has become a real issue in the most surprising variety of Western churches. The response to one sentence in the World Council's Accra Statement, *Baptism, Eucharist and Ministry,* which, when dealing with the differences between pedobaptist and 'believers' baptism' traditions, calls attention to the anomaly of baptizing children but not admitting them to eucharist[1], helped stimulate an already existing process to the extent that a consultation on young and the eucharist was held at Bad Segeberg in the Spring of 1980.[2] In one Anglican Province after another provincial doctrinal commissions argue that the present separation in time of baptism and the first reception of the eucharist is without theological defence and that the anomaly ought to be righted in the production of new baptismal liturgies.[3] This may at first cause consternation but, at least in some provinces, it is happening.

What I would like to do in this Study is first to look at the practice of the patristic church, then to look at several medieval and reformation discussions of the question, and, finally, to ask what all of this has to say to the pastoral and sacramental life of the church today. In Appendix 1 I have added a note on progress in the Anglican Communion. In addition, because of the English provenance of the Study (though my own is Canada), and because of its relevance in the Church of England today, Colin Buchanan has added as a further appendix a brief survey of the position in that Church.

David Holeton

---

[1] *One Baptism, One Eucharist and a Mutually Recognized Ministry* (W.C.C.), 'Baptism' V.B. 18. 'Those churches which baptize children, but refuse them a share in the eucharist before confirmation, may wish to ponder whether they have fully appreciated and accepted the consequences of infant baptism.'

[2] The papers and consensus statement are to be published in a Faith and Order Paper of the W.C.C.

[3] See my survey of the literature in *Studia Liturgica* XII, 2-3 (1977) p.129 ff. and Appendix 1 on pp.25-26 below.

1. BEGINNINGS

It is fair to say that the origins of infant baptism are, and will likely remain, obscure. The great Jeremias-Aland debate of a generation ago left pedobaptists convinced of the antiquity of their practice and those who hold to believers' baptism convinced that pedobaptism is a practice that is without either scriptural or apostolic warrant[1], although there are considerably more signs today than there were at the time of the debate itself that each side has gained considerably more appreciation of the other's rationale for its practice.[2]

The data that can be presented to prove that the apostolic church communicated infants is as circumstantial as that which proves she baptized them. Nobody is likely to be won one way or another. Three brief examples occur. The first two are of inclusive language in the context of the baptismal eucharist. That is, both Justin[3] and Hippolytus[4] speak of the baptismal eucharist in such a way that all those who have been baptized must also be seen as receiving the eucharist immediately after their baptism. On the basis of these texts there are some who would argue that it was inconceivable to either Justin or Hippolytus that one could be initiated into the body of Christ without receiving both baptism and the eucharist.[5] In the Hippolytan text one would then have the primary source for the practice in a whole variety of Church Orders, particularly in the East, should the practice not have already have existed. It is in that area, however, that we still have insufficient data to risk dating the beginning of the practice.[6] Here there is still an area of darkness.

The other example is archaeological and joins the ranks of Zosimus and similar epigraphs of children who died in infancy after having received emergency baptism. Julia Florentina, died, aged 18 months 22 days, having received emergency baptism at 2 a.m. But because she did not die immediately after her baptism she was given the eucharist again four hours later.[7] Here again one has a text very much of the type used by Jeremias to prove the case for pedobaptism. It is convincing only if you accept the oblique reference to the sacrament *('ita ut consueta repeterit')* and if you accept the baptism and communion of an infant *in extremis* as having something to do with the normal sacramental life of

---

[1] J. Jeremias *Infant Baptism in the First Four Centuries* (S.C.M., London, 1960): J. Jeremias *The Origins of Infant Baptism* (S.C.M., London, 1963).

[2] The W.C.C. consultation at Louisville (*Faith and Order Paper* No. 97) made considerable gains in a Baptist acceptance of infant baptism in the context of a living community of faith. Cf. pp.101ff.

[3] 1 *Apol.* 61, 10-12.

[4] G. J. Cuming, *Hippolytus: A Text for Students* (Grove Liturgical Study No. 8, Grove Books, 1976) p.21.

[5] M. Jourjon, 'Quatre conseils pour un bon usage des pères en sacramentaire' in *Maison-Dieu* 119 (1974) pp.75-76.

[6] cf. J. Jeremias *Infant Baptism in the First Four Centuries*, pp.73ff., for the parallel argument on infant baptism.

[7] Diehl, 1549.

4

the church. If you are convinced by this sort of text then you have grounds from which the later, more readily documented, practice has obviously grown. If not, you are in the company of a goodly number from the past who see the whole practice as dating from the time of Cyprian. In either case, let me suggest once again that the texts, although fewer in number, are very much of the same type as were Jeremias' in his case for infant baptism.

Having said that, let me turn rather briefly to two men who give us incontestable witness to the establishment of the practice. Cyprian gives us what appears to be an already developed theology of the practice as well as several illustrations of infant communion. First, he bears witness to the coupling of John 3.5 ('Unless a man be born again of water and the Spirit . . .') and John 6.53 ('Unless you eat the flesh of the Son of Man . . .') as a single *logion* in the *traditio fidei,* establishing what is necessary for participation in the Christian community.[1] Infants are as capable of baptism as are adults and share equally in the divine gift given in baptism.[2] Having thus been baptized in the Spirit the newborn drink thereon from the Lord's cup[3], and are thus both 'baptized and sanctified' *('baptizandum et sanctificandum').*[1] It is baptism and eucharist which establish membership in the Christian community. Membership in the community thereafter depends, for Cyprian, on continued participation in the eucharist. The two fabulous accounts of infants and a young girl in *De Lapsis* illustrate this.[5] In both these well-known incidents it is clear that infants and children establish membership in a particular religious community by participation in its rites. The infants who were taken by their parents to share in the pagan sacrifices can only plead at the last day 'It was not we who did anything, nor of ourselves that we left the Lord's food and drink . . .'.[6] The little girl taken by her nurse to pagan sacrifices could not later physically receive the eucharist—'the eucharist could not remain in a body or a mouth that was defiled . . .'.[7]

The incident may be difficult to credit, but it reveals Cyprian's conviction that participation in the eucharist establishes one's identity as a Christian just as participation in the pagan sacrifices was necessary to fulfil one's identification with those cultic acts.[8] Thus for Cyprian the eucharist is as necessary for the christian as is baptism, and for both sacraments age is unimportant. Baptism and the eucharist are inseparable and for Cyprian it is the eucharist that creates the Christian community. To abandon the eucharist is to abandon the community and to abandon either is to abandon Christ.

[1] Cyprian *Ad Quirinum* III, 25.
[2] Cyprian *Ep. 64.* passim: *Ep. 69,* XIII 3-XIV.1.
[3] Cyprian *Ep. 63,* VIII.3.
[4] Cyprian *Ep. 64,* II.a.
[5] Cyprian, *De Lapsis* 9 and 25.
[6] Cyprian *De Lapsis* 9.
[7] Cyprian *De Lapsis* 25.
[8] cf. Eusebius *De Mart. Palest.* 9; H. Leclercq *Les certificats de sacrifice païen, sous Dèce, en 250,* (Paris, 1914) pp.4, 35.

It is Augustine who gives us the most extensive theological reflection on infants and the eucharist. This is not simply a result of the polemic of the Pelagian controversy, as his interest in the matter antedates his contact with that question and it operates in two quite different areas. First, Augustine breaks with the tradition, used almost invariably in the patristic literature, which sees the infant as innocent and without malice. In that tradition infancy was held up as a model for what we would see as its sentimental qualities. The obvious poverty of an infant is used by John Chrysostom as a model of the absolute poverty of the Christian before God.[1] The *Shepherd* of Hermas exhorts the reader to be simple and innocent so that like babies he will not know the evil that destroys the lives of men.[2] Leo sees infancy as the mistress of humility, the rule of innocence and the model of gentleness. It is something towards which Christ directs men and to which he calls back the aged.[3]

Augustine will have none of that. For him all that is to be found in an adult is to be found present and operative in the infant. 'It is the physical weakness of the baby that makes it seem innocent, not the quality of its inner life.'[4] It is for this reason that Augustine insists that they too need a Saviour.[5]

It is here, however that Augustine does what we would not necessarily expect, he makes the infant the model of the perfect subject for the sacraments. This is in part because the infant images the total helplessness of the human condition. The human creature must come to the Father with the same helpless abandon as the sucking infant does to his mother.[6] Yet there is another dimension to Augustine's use of the infant as the model of the perfect sacramental subject. It is that of the pre-rational, or the non-rational, as the ideal approach to the sacrament. The words with which Jesus reveals the mystery of the eucharist in John 6 are those of infants or the mad.[7] To eat the sacrament is to become a child inwardly. In other words Augustine sees as ideal subjects for the sacraments the two categories of persons we have traditionally excluded: infants and the insane.

Here, the normal criteria by which we judge sacramental capability are ignored. We come to understand this only if we can free ourselves from the equation of chronology, cerebral achievement and Christian maturity. Augustine, like his contemporaries saw a radical disjuncture between age and Christian maturity. 'For you know that all who are baptized, whether they are old or young are called infants.'[8]

[1] *In Matthaeum* 15, 1-2.
[2] *Shepherd.* Precept II, 1.
[3] *Sermo* 3-4.
[4] *Confessions* I, vii, II.
[5] *Serm.* 174, 6; *Lib. IV. Cont. Jul.* III, 2; *de Peccat. Mer. et Remis.* III, 4, 7.
[6] *en in Ps.* 54, 24; *Conf. IV,* i, I.
[7] *en in Ps.* 33 II, 1.
[8] *Tract. in Joh.* XXVI, 1.

Baptism becomes the great equalizer: age, national and social status are literally washed away and men become brothers, one people, and infants.[1] And as with infants their diet becomes milk and honey.[2]

Augustine, then, develops a theology in which the communion of infants is both logical and necessary. He builds on the tradition he finds in Cyprian repeatedly using the two verses from John as a couplet.[3] The idea of the eucharist as the sacrament of unity which constitutes the church pervades his writings. But to this he adds a theology of both rationality and chronology that, given the reaction to the Pelagian crisis, assures the right of infants to communion the same status as their right to baptism. This position finds itself confirmed in both synodical[4] and papal[5] action.

[1] Zeno of Verona *Tract.* I, 24, 1; 38, 1.
[2] Jerome *In Esiam,* LV, 1-2.
[3] Augustine *De Peccat. Mer. et Remis,* I, 24, 34.
[4] *Ep. Milvetan Council to Innocent 2, 3 (PL* 33, 763).
[5] Innocent I *Ep.* 182, 5.

2. DEVOLUTION

I do not intend to trace the devolution of the practice of infant communion in the west. Canon J. D. C. Fisher has done the best study of the question available in English which is published in the Alcuin Club's Collection No. 47.[1] Let me simply say that the baptismal communion of infants remained normative in the Western church until the twelfth century. Its disappearance can be directly attributed to four factors: first, the separation of baptism from the eucharist; second, the separation of the chalice and the laity; third, the injunction against reservation under two kinds; and finally, the factor that makes all this possible, the loss of any sense among both religious and the laity that communion was a normal part of the mass.

As baptismal communion waned it did not always vanish without trace. Like the Cheshire cat, it often left a smile of what once was. Sometimes this was liturgical. Rituals were left with rubrics directing the newly baptized to be brought to the altar when they would have received communion, but nothing then happened; sometimes they were given the ablutions, or a sip of unconsecrated wine.[2] Sometimes, where the liturgy had lost any vestige of the practice, folk-piety provided substitute rites: in Carinthia the newly baptized had wheat soaked in wine placed in their mouths; the silver spoon given as a baptismal gift is likely to be a much-removed reminder of the practice long-gone.[3]

---

[1] cf. Chapter 6 'The Separation of Communion from Initiation' p.101 ff.
[2] cf. P-M Gy 'Die Taufkommunion der kleiner Kinder in der lateinischen Kirche' in H. Auf der Maur *Zeichen des Glaubens* (Einsiedeln, 1972) pp.485-491.
[3] I owe this theory to a conversation with Prof. Balthasar Fischer.

3. RESTORATION: (i) BOHEMIA

I would like to turn now to two reformation restorations of the practice as I believe they have much to say to the present situation in the church. The first of these occurred in Bohemia.

In 1414 Jakoubek of Stribro restored the chalice to the laity of Prague. Within three years Utraquists were communicating infants. Within four years the practice was the first of the 23 Hussite Articles. After that the practice was one which was insisted on in every attempt at reconciliation between Catholics and Utraquists.

We need to ask how such a practice could so quickly become of such importance in the most radical reform movement of the middle ages. The answer lies at the levels of popular piety, communal experience, and theology.

In the late fourteenth century Bohemia witnessed the most significant popular eucharistic movement of the high middle ages. Initiated by Jan Milic of Kromeríz[1] and given its theological rationale by Matthias of Janov[2] the movement sought to restore frequent, best daily, communion. Unlike the Belgian[3] movement of the preceding century the Bohemian movement was not concerned with devotion towards the sacrament as such, but rather that the whole people of God ought to be fed regularly not only for the welfare of their own souls but also for the reform of society as a whole.[4]

In attempting to promote frequent communion Matthias had to make a number of points to combat the popular eucharistic theology of the time; thus he had to argue that the eucharist is common to all just as it is necessary to all[5], that it cannot be received by the priest on behalf of the laity[6], and that it ought to be received often not just by a clerical or spiritual élite, but also by the poor and by the *parvuli in Christo.*[7] Baptism leads to eucharist[8], and those who are in communion with the church through baptism ought also to remain in communion through the eucharist.[9]

---

[1] 1325-1374. There is a 'Vita Milicii' in *Fontes rerum bohemicarum [FRB]* I, pp.403-430: his tract 'Gracie dei', on frequent communion is preserved in Vlastimil Kybal ed., *Matthiae de Janov dicti magister Parisiensis,* II, (Innsbrück and Prague, 1909) pp.98-102.

[2] c.1355-1393. The most accessible work on Matthias is V. Kybal, 'Etude sur les origines du mouvement hussite en Bohême. Matthias de Janov.' in *Revue historique* CIII (1910), pp.8-31. His one great work *Regulae veteris et novi testament* is edited by V. Kybal, *Matthias de Janov . . .5* vols. (1-IV Innsbrück and Prague 1908-1913, V Prague 1926).

[3] cf. C. Lambot 'L'office de la Fée-Dieu. Aperçus nouveaux sur les origines' in *Revue Bénédictine* 54 (1942) pp.61-123.

[4] Matthias de Janov *Regulae . . .,* Kybal V, p.139.

[5] *Regulae,* I, p.72.

[6] *Regulae,* II, p.26.

[7] *Regulae,* I, p.87.

[8] *Regulae,* V, p.136.

[9] *Regulae,* V, p.35.

The images Matthias uses for the eucharist are not common for his time. His concern is not primarily the eucharistic sacrifice but rather the eucharistic body of 1 Corinthians 10.17 becoming the renewed society of believers. This, for his time, was not at all common among reformers.[1] Matthias' views caused considerable concern in Bohemia although his position was given support by a number of influential individuals.[2] Frequent communion was not, however, to win the day. In 1388 theologians and lawyers of the University of Prague condemned frequent communion and declared that it ought to be received, at the most, once a month.[3] In 1389 Matthias was made to recant.

His recantation, however, had little effect on the spread of his ideas on frequent communion.[4] Thomas of Stitné, a member of the petty nobility in Southern Bohemia who attended lectures at the university in Prague, issued a series of devotional books, in the vernacular, on family religion. In them the idea of frequent communion is promoted for the laity.[5] Groups practising frequent communion began to appear in Prague and throughout Bohemia.[6] By the end of the fourteenth century there was a broad base of support for frequent communion within the realm.

At first we have no particular information about the age of those admitted to communion. Matthias does not specifically advocate the communion of newly baptized infants although he is aware of the practice in the early church[7] and sees baptism as implying eucharist[8] in that all those who are baptized, unless they are in a state of serious sin, normally constitute the eucharistic community.[9] In the same way Matthias does not concern himself with the reception of the chalice by the laity, but the idea is latent in what he says and only time is necessary before the idea becomes obvious to all who read his *Regulae*. It is in this sense that Matthias is the formative theologian of the Hussite church.

[1] For a useful survey of reform movements in the middle ages see Malcolm Lambert *Medieval Heresy* (London, 1977). Reform movements of the time tended to reject rather than encourage sacramental practices.

[2] A number are listed in a contemporary codex, cf. 'De communione quotidiane' in Karl Höfler, *Geschichtschreiber der Husitischen in Böhmen,* II (Vienna, 1865) pp.60-61.

[3] 'Retractio M. Matthiae' in Frantisek Palacky *Documenta Mag. Joannis Hus* (Prague, 1869) p.700.

[4] Matthias in fact continued to preach and write in favour of frequent communion despite two recantations.

[5] *Regulae,* V, p.33 ff.

[6] The Bethlehem Chapel continued to agitate for reform at the popular level and the university continued to expose those who were to have more widespread influence to these reforming ideas. Henry of Bitterfeld, the German Dominican who held a chair at the university continued to advocate frequent communion, as did Matthew of Cracow.

[7] *Regulae,* V, p.231.

[8] *Regulae,* V, p.136.

[9] *Regulae,* V, p.33ff.

In 1414 Jakoubek of Stríbro restored the chalice to the laity. When he challenged in the matter by Andrew of Brod[1] Jakoubek replies that the idea came to him as a revelation.[2] By this, he says he means from a study of Scripture and the Fathers. What has happened is that one of the ideas implicit in Matthias has become obvious and enacted. It does not take long before the second idea, that is, the communion of all the baptized, becomes an issue. It already appears in the debate between Andrew of Brod and Jakoubek[3], but the idea still seems to be theoretical rather than an actual practice. By the next year the question has become a matter of such vigorous debate within university circles that the question could not be included in the declaration on the feast of the Conversion of St. Paul, 1417, which attempted a conservative definition of the principles of reform. That same year we know from a letter of complaint by the conservative Stephen of Dolnay that the practice existed.[4]

Once the practice was introduced it seems to have become accepted quickly, although not without opposition.[5] The scriptural proof-texts for the practice join those for other Hussite reforms on the walls of Bethlehem Chapel[6] and the Synod of St. Wenceslas held to end internal dissent the following year listed the communion of infants as the first of its 23 Articles.[7]

Within a matter of months the mercurial Wenceslas reversed his policy and pursued a policy hostile to the communion of infants while continuing to tolerate utraquism.[8] What is interesting is that the change of policy results not only in rhetoric[9], but also in popular

[1] Andrew of Brod 'Disputatio Academica contra Jacobum de Misa' in Herman von der Hardt (ed.) *Magnum Oecumenicum Constantiense Concilium III* (Leipzig, 1698) col. 392 ff.

[2] Jakoubek of Stríbro 'Vindiciae contra Andrae Brodam' in *Hardt,* III col. 566.

[3] *Hardt,* III col. 406-407, 421 ff., 431 ff.

[4] Stephen of Dolnay 'Epistolae ad Hussitas' in Bernard Pez, *Thesaurus Anecdotorum Novissimus IV,* (Augsburg, 1723) col. 509, 576, 656, 668.

[5] Lord Cenek opposed the practice and his chaplain, Peter Cendát, wrote a treatise against it. (Cod. *Bibl. Univ.* IV. H. 17 fols, 192-204). John Jesenic and Simon of Tisnov opposed the practice from the University cf. Frantisek M. Bartos *Literární Cinnost M. Jakoubka ze Stríbra* (Prague, 1925) Nos. 71, 72, 74. It is interesting to note, however, that the matter is not listed in the letter of Martin V to Wenceslas among the 24 steps to be taken to make reconciliation possible (Höfler, II, pp.240-243). One may safely assume that this is either oversight or that word of the practice had not reached the papal chancery rather than any favourable papal disposition on the matter. Here the *Longa Epistola Elenchtica* of the 'Anonymous Theologian at Constance' (Hardt, III, col. 366-7) seems to be an unreliable witness to just what the Council knew of what was taking place in Bohemia.

[6] Bohumil Ryba *Betlemské texty* (Prague, 1951) pp141-162. Fragments of the texts were discovered during the restoration of the chapel in the 1950s.

[7] Palacký *Documenta,* p.678.

[8] 'Anonymus de origine Taboritum' in Höfler, I, 528.

[9] Jacoubek wrote his 'Listek o Primluvu ukrále—Response to the King; that Infant Communion Should not be Suppressed (Bartos, *Literárni Cinnost,* No. 75). Text in F. M. Bartos *Do ctyr prazkých artukulu* (Prague, 1925) n.101.

demonstrations in favour of the practice. A mob confronts Wenceslas in Prague and through Nicholas of Hus they petition for a change in this hostile attitude.[1] For his efforts Nicholas was dismissed from court and banned from Prague and the crowds continued to agitate, and apparently, except where forcibly restrained, continued their practice.

At the same time another type of reaction was taking place. While Prague was large enough to contain several theological camps and there was a certain freedom to maintain Hussite practice in at least a few parishes the situation was different in the countryside.[2] There the vigour with which the king's new policy was enforced depended heavily on the sympathies of the local patrons and magistrates.[3] Patrons with Hussite sympathies were less inclined to enforce the law than were their Catholic counterparts. In the archdeaconry of Bechyne, around the towns of Usti, Pisek, and Bechyne Castle, the reaction to the new royal policy was revolution.

Peasants, led by utraquist priests who had been expelled from their cures left their farms and villages and gathered on a mountain, not far from Bechyne which they renamed Tabor after the mountain of the Transfiguration. There, says a Chronicle, they came 'to hear and obey the Word of God and to take communion freely, with their children too, in the glorious sacrament of the body and blood of Christ.'[4] The movement quickly grew and in a quarter of a year the Taborites numbered 50,000 'not counting women and children.'[5] Assemblies continued regularly—it is not clear whether they managed to assemble every week, but it is clear that festivals were kept with particular devotion, and that the whole community present constituted the eucharistic body.[6]

From the first assembly on Tabor on Easter Day 1419 until the end of the Hussite movement the position of infant communion was assured. After the Defenestration and the importation of foreign mercenaries to eliminate all religious deviation Taborites were prepared to die rather than abandon the practice.[1] In each succeeding alliance between the

---

[1] Laurence of Brezová 'Historia Hussitica' in *FRB,* V, p.345.

[2] Wenceslas allowed Utraquist celebration in private houses and at any side altars to which the Utraquists had access; in addition they were allowed three churches for public worship.

[3] Jan Zelivský's sermon of 28 May 1419 indicates that some patrons were particularly zealous in enforcing this new policy. Text in Amadeo Molnár *Jan Zelivsky* (Prague, 1953) pp.139ff.

[4] A historical passage in the Czech speech opening the Hussite Diet of 12 January 1426, and quoted in Howard Kaminsky *A History of the Hussite Revolution* (Berkeley, 1967) pp.279-80.

[5] 'Anonymus de origine Taboritarum' in Höfler, I, p.528

[6] Laurence of Breznová *FRB* v, pp.334 f, 345; 'Chronicon causam sacerdotum Thaboriensium continens in Höfler, II, p.482 ff.

[7] The best known of these Utraquist passions is the burning of the parish priest of Arnostovice, together with peasants and children who refused to recant, in July 1420 by the troops of Duke of Austria. Ernest Denis *Huss et la guerre des Hussites* (Paris 1878/1930) p.248.

conservatives of Prague and the Taborites, infant communion was a principle without which the Taborites would not enter the alliance. And so it remained.

Celebrations of the eucharist were the life and soul of the popular religion of the Hussites. In their own tongue they sang:

'You gave us his body to eat,
His holy blood to drink.
What more could he have done for us?

Let us not deny it to little children
Nor forbid them
When they eat Jesus' body.

Of such is the kingdom of heaven
As Christ himself told us,
And holy David says also:

"From the mouths of small children
And of all innocent babes
Has come forth God's praise
That the adversary may be cast down."

* * *

Praise God, you children
You tiny babes,
For he will not drive you away,
But feed you on his holy body.'

The time comes to ask why such a practice came to be seen as such a pivotal issue in what was perhaps the most significant revolution of the high middle ages. Obviously there is first the great passion that is engendered by not only doing what you believe to be right but by doing what the Lord himself commanded. This is easily understandable with utraquism and Utraquists continually refer to the practice as being 'According to the institution of the Lord', but this is rather more difficult to say about the communion of infants.

The insistence that John 6.53-4 ought not to be understood only in a spiritual sense[1] was a crucial argument for the frequent communion of the laity in the face of an exegetical tradition that had allowed only a spiritual exegesis of the text. If the text is to be understood in a literal as well as a spiritual sense—that is, while we do not actually eat the physical body of Christ but rather we eat his body spiritually but the means of that eating is sacramental—then there is only a very small step to be taken to insisting that *all the laity share in the sacramental meal*. This step is essentially forced on the reader by Matthias when he poses the question 'if you are in communion with the church in the first manner [qui abscisus est a communione primo modo], that is through baptism, why not also in the second [abscius est quoad participacionem vite e spiritus eciam a secunda]?'[2]

[1] *Regulae*, II, p.32.
[2] *Regulae*, V, p.38.

This in itself, however, would not necessarily move the reader to the idea that infants should be included in the eucharistic meal. It would be very easy to introduce grounds on which qualification for the sacrament might be granted. 1 Corinthians 11.27-29 would, for instance, have been a very facile proof-text to invoke in order to exclude infants. This, however, Matthias does not do, and I would suggest it is because the objects of his argument are the poor and the disenfranchized, the *parvuli in Christo;* those who in their simplicity might well not be able to 'discern the body' in any articulate manner. It is the simplest of the *plebs Dei* who are also to be renewed to become the new society. These are the people who are to be nourished daily, like children, on the milk of the eucharist.[1] To suggest any grounds for qualification for this nourishment other than baptism is unthinkable. The child thus becomes the image of the perfect communicant.

Having inherited this tradition and having begun to communicate infants, what gives the practice such tenacity? Is it simply Czech bloody-mindedness in the face of opposition, another rallying point like the lay chalice, or is it something more? It would appear as if several factors are operative here and each nourishes the others. When the rural Utraquists were excluded from their parishes and the Taborite movement began, particularly with its chiliastic undertones, there was an entirely new experience of religious community. Not only did the members of this new community have the common experience of expulsion from their own parishes as a basis for their new society, an exodus as it were, but they were obliged to look after one another's needs. there was a solidarity that had not previously existed.

In his *Chronicle* Laurence of Brezova[2] tells us that priests and villagers from the surrounding area came to Tabor as a sign of solidarity with those already there, and for the consolation and comfort of the brothers and sisters who were staying there. Those gathered on Tabor led a communal life. All things were held in common, expenses were paid from the common treasury, and the system of government was through popularly elected aldermen and officials. Those who went to Tabor were determined to build a society on new principles, in which the poor would have a full share in the community.[3] This, in part, was to be effected by the whole community sharing in the eucharist. The sacrament was seen to effect what it signified. In this light it would be as natural to feed children and infants at the eschatological meal as it would be to make them a part of the new creation in baptism.

[1] *Regulae,* V, p.59f.
[2] *FRB,* V, p.400f.
[3] Josef Macek *Tábor v Husitském Revolucnìm, Zvok* (Prague 1952, 1955) presents a massive sociological study of the population of Tábor. It is clear that the poor and the dispossessed that flocked there in the thousands shared in a life in which they had both material and social benefits greater than they had ever known. Unfortunately Macek's study is seriously marred by a complete misunderstanding of the religious nature of the community and is intent on producing an historical analysis based only on the class struggle.

In all of this the academic debate of the Prague masters is secondary although not without its importance. The practice once begun was so infectious among radical Utraquists that it needed no academic justification. The numerous tracts on the subject tended to justify the practice on scriptural and historical grounds.[1] The couplet of John 3.5 and John 6.53 was invoked along with 1 Corinthians 10.17. The text of Dionysius[2] saying that no sacrament was complete without the eucharist often headed a sizeable patristic florilege. The masters were also aware that infants received communion in the Eastern rites[3] and had first hand contact with the Byzantine rite through the Monastery of Emmaus in Prague refounded and patronized by Charles IV. They also knew that the practice had been a part of the Western liturgy until the recent past[4] and at least in some Bohemian rituals there were still liturgical vestiges that were obviously such.[5]

What this has to say to the church today is this. Any church that begins to encourage frequent communion among the laity in the context of a piety that sees the eucharist as a communal action rather than as an action done on the behalf of a collection of individuals cannot help but pose new questions as to who is to be included in the eucharistic community. Once the community becomes one in which all are accepted in its corporate life despite age, or intelligence, or social status, the question of universal participation in the eucharist becomes a real one. Once all the community shares in the eucharist the experience becomes a conversion. You can never be as you were before. This is what happened to the Hussites; and this is what is happening in some churches today.

---

[1] cf. Jacoubek 'De communione parvulorum' in Ryba, *loc. cit.;* John of Rokycana 'Argumenta pro communuone parvulorum' in Prague *Bibl. Nat.* V. 22 fol. 293[r]-297[r]; John of Pribram 'Ad honorem dom. Jesu . . .' in *Bib. Nat.* (Prague) V.G.6. fol. 1-84.

[2] *De eccles. hierarchia* 3, 1.

[3] cf. Anonymous Hussite Tract in Prague *Bibl. Cap.* D.CXVIII fol. 188[r] ff.

[4] cf. Anonymous Hussite Tract in Prague *Bibl. Cap.* D.CIX.2 fol. 199[r].

[5] In Prague *Bib. Nat.* VI. G. 7 fol. 32[r], after the giving of the candle the priest is required to say 'Sacramentum domini nostri Iesu Christi perficiat tibi in vitam aeternam.' There is no rubric directing what he should do in this, the last of a series of postbaptismal rites.

4. RESTORATION: (ii) ENGLAND

One of the more neglected aspects of the pedobaptist controversy that raged in this country during the seventeenth century is its treatment of the question of the communion of infants. An examination of this period is important for us because it faces us with a question that is still only partially resolved.

Discussion of the possibility of communicating infants and young children is almost as old as English Reformation literature itself. Thomas Cartwright raises the question in the *Replye* citing the practice as coeval with infant baptism and of Augustinian origin.[1] Whitgift totally ignores the question in his *Defense* and simply refuses to take issue with Cartwright over the necessity of baptism for salvation.[2] This was to be for quite some time the initial Anglican response whenever the question was raised: simply pretend the issue does not exist.

Cartwright does not push the question and it essentially lies dormant for sixty years except for an occasional mention in anti-Roman polemics[3] or catechetical material that tried to draw distinctions between baptism and eucharist in terms of order, frequency, opportunity, elements, and subject.[4] But as the country moves towards revolution and the baptismal and sacramental controversies become more bitter the question becomes increasingly important. With the Restoration the issue ceases to be taken seriously by most Anglicans and other pedobaptists.

In the baptismal debates the question of infants and the eucharist is one that is continually raised by anti-pedobaptists. In doing so they force those who defend the baptism of infants to clarify what had been two basically unexamined questions. The first involves the basic epistemology of baptism. The sacramental model inherited from the middle ages and used, basically without reflection, was biological. Baptism is the the sacrament of infancy, the new birth is something for babies, and it never occurs to the pedobaptist that others might possibly be candidates for that sacrament. The images used for baptism are those of passivity.[5] Baxter theologizes on this passivity claiming that it expresses a state of mind which was an assent in faith to the covenant and an expression of the reality of a saving faith.[6]

These images had worked well in a society in which church and state were one and in which there was no other sacramental model. When

---

[1] Thomas Cartwright *A Replye to an answere made of M. Doctor Whitegifte* . . . (London, 1573) pp.143-4.

[2] John Whitgift *The Defence of the Answere to the Admonition* (London, 1574).

[3] Thomas Morton *A Catholic Appeal for Protestants* (London, 1610) pp.136-8.

[4] Daniel Rogers *A Treatise of the two Sacraments* (London, 1633) pp.24-25.

[5] John Tombes *Anti-paedobaptism* (London, 1654) p.37, citing John Church; Francis Johnson *A brief treatise . . . against two errors of the Anabaptists* (London, 1645) pp.4-6.

[6] Richard Baxter *Plain Scripture Proofs of Infants Church-membership and Baptisme* (London, 1651) pp.114-5.

the model was challenged by those opposed to the baptism of infants as well as to a state church the model quickly collapse. If, said the antipedobaptists, baptism is the sacrament of birth and the eucharist is the sacrament of growth and progress, who are more fitting subjects to receive this second sacrament than those who are doing the most growing; infants and young children?[1]

For the time this was a very serious attack on the whole sacramental system. A model that had basically been accepted without question collapsed in a very short time. Faced with this attack no attempt was made to justify or defend the model.

With the biological point lost, pedobaptists retreat and construct new barricades to fence the eucharist from children. This involves a cerebral theology of the eucharist that treats the sacarament in purely spiritualized terms.What is interesting is that in achieving this new position they bypass, and are allowed to do so by their adversaries, any question of the relationship between the Lord's Supper and a meal. In the whole debate I have only found one instance where eating and drinking are taken seriously as signs of the eucharist and infants declared capable.[2] Even when the debate moves on to the question of the Passover this too is treated in spiritual terms where those who ate and drank had but drops and crumbs.

A new theology of the eucharist is constructed in terms of requirements, capacity, and faith. The first requirement was an aspect of the ascendancy of puritan political power and the much sought-after right of presbyters to examine and suspend communicants. An Act of Parliament passed on 20 October 1644 was a triumph for the intellectualization of the sacraments. Not only did the presbyter have the right to deny the eucharist to those who did not give tangible evidence of leading the godly life, he could also examine and suspend those who did not know enough about the faith. The effect of this was heavy on both the upper and lower classes. The former were generally incapable of leading the godly life and the latter could not possibly learn all that was required of them in the barrage of little hookies that were to be read and memorized by would-be communicants.[3] The result was to exclude both classes from the eucharist leaving a rather self-satisfied Puritan bourgeoisie.

[1] Tombes *loc. cit.*

[2] Thomas Blake *Infants Baptisme, freed from Antichristianisme* (London, 1644) p.95.

[3] e.g. J.B. *A Short Catechisme: Composed according to the Rules and Directions concerning Suspension from the Sacrament of The Lord's Supper, in case of ignorance. And published for ignorant people* (London 1645): Anon. *The Rules Directions of the Lords and Commons Assembled in Parliament: Concerning the Examination of all such as shall be admitted to the Sacrament of the Lord's Supper within the Kingdome of England . . . with Questions and Answers concerning the same* (London, 1646). A helpful introduction to the question of seventeenth century Presbyterian catechisms can be found in Alexander F. Mitchell *Catechisms of the Second Reformation* (London, 1886).

The reaction to this sacramental theology based on bourgeois morality and knowledge was to push the question of infants and the eucharist. Anglicans, anti-pedobaptists, and some puritans, all defended a more liberal policy of admission to the eucharist, but it was the challenge of the radicals that left both Anglican and Puritan alike gasping for breath.

Giles Firmin, poses the question this way:
> 'I saw Presbyteriall Brethren keep back half or three quarters of their Churches from the Lords Supper, and that for divers years together, yet did so constantly baptise their children, I thought with myself, where have these men a ground for this practice?'[1]

> 'To baptize is to give Communion, "baptise into one body," then there is Communion given with the body, by an excommunicated person: is not this a contradiction? Communion is most properly seen in Baptisme and the Lords Supper.'[2]

The Puritans had little to justify their pastoral practice. The baptism of infants was justified on the grounds that those being baptized were the infants of believers, the practice of indiscriminate infant baptism having been rejected. Yet those presenting their children for baptism were not (at least obviously) believers as they themselves had been barred from the eucharist. Pastoral practice sat ill with puritan ecclesiology.

Thomas Lambe, a Puritan, summarizes the problem:
> 'As Believers' Baptism agreeth to particular churches, gathered out of the world by the Word, so doth infant baptisme agree to the National Church, and Communion therein, . . . because by Baptisme they are immembered into the Church, and so capable of Church Communion; yea ('tis their right) if their Baptisme be reckoned valid, because according to Scripture, Acts 2.45, all baptised persons were added to the Church, and continued in the Apostles' fellowship, breaking bread and prayer: by what rule then can the Parishes be withdrawn from, when they are esteemed duly baptised persons, till legally proceeded against for disorderly walking.'[3]

In this vein there was a general agreement that baptized infants had a right to the eucharist but not a right in it, Unwittingly drawing on the Thomistic distinction between *jus ad rem* and *jus in re*.[4] This distinction, however, seemed to carry little weight even among those who were trying to find a rationale for refusing the eucharist to children.

---

[1] Giles Firmin *A Sober Reply to the Sober Answer of Reverend Mr. Cawdrey* (London, 1653) p.56 (misnumbered 54).

[2] Firmin *A Sober Reply . . .* p.37.

[3] Thomas Lambe *Truth prevailing against the fiercest opposition* (London, 1655) Foreword, n.p.

[4] John Brinsley *The Doctrine and Practice of Paedobaptisme asserted and vindicated* (London, 1645) pp.34-5.

Stephen Marshall, a puritan and strong defender of infant baptism, summarized the developing question this way:

> '. . . if [children] being capable of the spiritual part, must intitle them to the outward signe, why then doe we not also admit them to the Sacrament of the Lords Supper, which is the seale of the Covenant of Grace, as well as the Sacrament of Baptisme? And this is urged, the rather because the Infants of the Jewes did eat of the Passover, as well as were circumcised, now if our Infants have every way as large a priviledge as the Infants of the Jewes had then we cannot deny them the same privilege which their Infants had, and consequently they must partake of the one Sacrament, as well as the other.'[1]

The farther Puritans entered into the debate the more their position became untenable. One of the principal arguments they had used for the baptism of infants was the parallel between circumcision and baptism. Each was necessary to participation in its respective covenant, and covenant was the operative term in Puritan sacramental theology. Yet when radical theologians extended the parallel to Passover and the Supper the puritans could do little other than acknowledge the weakness of their position.

A few argued that the children of the Jews had never eaten the Passover or that

> 'If infants did partake of it, it was as a common meele to them and no Sacrament, as now they may eat of that bread, and drink of that wine, which is prepared for the Lords Supper, though not in the way of a Sacrament'.[2]

But most Puritan theologians were not prepared to reduce participation in the Supper to pure subjective activity

There are attempts made to find other grounds for refusing the eucharist to infants: no active faith and inability to examine themselves being the principal arguments used. These, however, are in time abandoned. If the baptizand need not comply with scripture and repent and openly confess the faith then the demand for self-examination cannot be made to exclude those baptized without personal repentance and confession.

Richard Baxter dealt the final blow to the debate over types of faith required for baptism and the eucharist. For Baxter they are one and the same.

> 'All that are meet subjects for Baptism, are (after their Baptism, without any further inward qualification, at least without another species of faith) meet subjects for the Lords Supper.'[3]

The question is all but settled.

[1] Stephen Marshall *A Sermon of the Baptizing of Infants* (London, 1644) p.51.
[2] Blake *Infants Baptisme* p.95.
[3] Richard Baxter *Certain Disputations of Right to Sacraments* (London, 1651).

Baxter had argued that the passivity of baptism expresses a state of mind which was an assent in faith to the covenant and an expression of the present reality of a saving faith. So too then, is the reply, are the actions of taking, eating and drinking. If passivity is the sign of the thing professed in one case then so is it in the other.

The final Baptist attack which defeats Baxter is the pairing of the couplet of 1 Corinthians 11.27-29 with 10.17. If the text on examination is proof for the exclusion of infants from the eucharist then the text on sharing in the one loaf is proof that these same infants are excluded from the body of Christ as a whole.[1] This Baxter cannot admit and simply asks for further proof from the Baptists that he should be communicating infants:

> 'I have fully proved that Infants must be baptized; Let them prove that they must receive the Lords Supper if they can: If they bring but as good proof for this, as I have done for the former, I shall heartily yield that they ought to receive both: Till then, it lies on them, and not on me; they that affirm that Infants should have the Lords Supper must prove it; they cannot expect that I should prove the Negative.'[2]

That, however, had essentially been done. In his *Discourse of the Liberty of Prophesying* Jeremy Taylor gave the question the most extensive examination it was to have during the century. Taylor had the luxury of watching the debate somewhat as an outsider. The polemic was directed against the Puritan establishment and Taylor, having already lost everything, could analyze the merits of the debate in a disinterested fashion. Not only does he bring something new to the debate but his conclusions are as surprising as they are unacceptable to both puritan and radical.

Taylor's Anglicanism obliges him to examine the queston historically as well as in a purely scriptural light. As such, he is the first to take the history of the practice seriously. He examines the patristic evidence and concludes that the practice is as ancient and as well founded as is infant baptism. His contemporaries had either refused to take serious account of the historical data when it was presented[3], or declared it a fabrication[4], or dismissed it as excessive Augustinianism.[5]

Taylor's theological conclusions are that infants ought to receive either both sacraments or neither.[6] But later, with the return of Anglican hegemony, he suggests that since the practice of infant communion has characterized the life of the church in particular ages and has not

[1] Henry Haggar *The Foundation of the Font Discovered* (London 1653) pp.66-67.
[2] Baxter *Certain Disputations* . . .p.114.
[3] Stephen Marshall *A Defense of Infant Baptism* (London, 1646) p.240.
[4] Samuel Chidley *A Christmas Plea for Infants to Baptisme* (London, 1644) p.87.
[5] John Tombes *Anti-Paedobaptism: or the Third Part* (London, 1657) p.885.
[6] Jeremy Taylor *Of the Liberty of Prophesying* (London, 1648) pp.232-3.

been a question that has attracted a division according to theological schools or camps the church has the right to withhold the eucharist from infants as being an unnecessary practice and one that would be better left alone during his time for the sake of the peace of the church.[1] But in so doing, Taylor suggests, a name ought to be invented for those who refuse to give communion to infants that is as disparaging as is Anabaptist for those who refuse to give them baptism.[2] There is no further attempt made by Puritans to create new obstacles for infant communion. Their ecclesiology basically does not admit a *jus ecclesia* that is independent of the *jus scriptura*. They have lost, and they know it.

Political events, however, did not allow the question to come to its natural end. Restoration inclusiveness brushed the question aside. Anglican comprehensiveness once again ignored what could be justified by scripture, theology, and tradition. The question, however, did not die. It needed to bide time. It was left to the later Non-jurors, who had contact with this earlier debate as well as a fascination for the East and the primitive, to restore infant communion.

The debate as a whole is much more significant than it may at first seem. What it has done for the tradition of English theology is three things. First, it has undermined the biological model of the sacraments. There is no necessary relationship between age and any particular sacrament; baptism is no more for babies than marriage is for teenagers. Second, it clarified the question of sacramental capability. Infants are as capable as are adults of receiving the eucharist. If they can receive the one they can receive the other. The attempt to legislate who was capable of receiving the eucharist (the pure and the literate) demonstrated the untenability of creating barriers to the sacraments. And, finally, the debate introduced a communal aspect into the sacramental debate that had completely fallen aside during the middle ages and had not been recovered by the English reformers.

Each of these questions was hard won in the midst of bitter religious controversy. And once won, the points were only slowly admitted. In fact, each point needs to be re-made today.

---

[1] *The Worthy Communicant* (London, 1661 (III, ii)).
[2] Taylor *Liberty* pp.232-3.

5. THE COMMUNION OF INFANTS AND YOUNG CHILDREN TODAY

What then does all of this have to say to us today? I have already said that the communion of young children has become an important question in the churches. Where it has been introduced it has been well received. The question of the communion of infants is being treated with somewhat more caution, yet where the practice has been introduced it soon becomes natural and a reversal of policy unthinkable. Yet the questions posed by the past must be answered.

While we have spent much time in recent years debating the place of confirmation in Christian initiation we have spent very little time over the exact role of the eucharist in initiation. While there is general agreement (except in England) that baptism admits to the eucharist, no one has dared ask whether or not those who are baptized but have not received the eucharist are really initiated into the body of Christ. I would suggest that the answer we could get from Justin, Hippolytus, Cyprian, and Augustine, would be, no, they are not. It is only when the question is pushed towards the absurd, like in the case of the man who died at the Paschal Vigil after baptism but before the eucharist, that we get a different answer.[1]

There is a high degree of correlation between the frequency with which the eucharist is received, the sense of community, and the communion of young children and infants. Each nourishes the other. It is perhaps not surprising then to see the question of infant communion being raised in churches where the parish eucharist is the norm and eucharistic community is taken seriously both within and outside the actual eucharistic celebration.

It is here that Cyprian and Augustine need to be taken seriously. If the eucharist is the weekly constitutive act of the church, and if participation in that eucharist signifies both our membership in the body and as such our allegiance to Christ himself, what are we doing when we baptize infants and young children and then refuse to admit them to the very act that both signifies and effects that membership?

It is here that we return to the issues raised during the seventeenth century debates. As I suggested earlier, these issues need once again to be clarified, and perhaps now can be in a way that was impossible, other than theoretically, during the debate itself.

First, most of us implicitly work with a biological model of the sacraments. Baptism is for babies, confirmation for the adolescent and the eucharist for the adult. Even our recent liturgies of Christian initiation make only a minimal accommodation for adult baptism. We are quite prepared to baptize, confirm, and admit an adult to the eucharist at a single celebration, but that event is the first liturgy we have to recognize his existence as we make no provision for a liturgy

[1] Fulgentius *Ep.* 12 no. 26 in *Corpus Christianorum* 91, pp.380-381.

that marks his entrance into any sort of catechumenate or any stages in his growth towards acceptance of Christ and the community and reciprocally the community's acceptance of him as a member. It is only in consciously abandoning the biological model that we can re-assess the admission of infants to the eucharist.

When we do this we have to reconsider both Augustine and Pelagius. We quite willingly accept Augustine's image of coming to God with the helplessness of a sucking child when we are speaking of baptism, yet, we balk when pressed to use the same image for speaking of the eucharist. But the image is as applicable to the one as it is to the other. When we come to the eucharist we become Pelagian in the wrong way. Instead of saying to each person 'for God's sake grow up', 'be perfect *[teleios]* as your Father in heaven is perfect', 'respond to God's initiative at the level at which you are capable,' for whatever sacrament is sought; we say, 'be a baby for baptism, but an adult for the eucharist.' This is both to misunderstand Augustine and to become a half-baked Pelagian.

Augustine's theological reflection on infants and the sacraments is not a theology of infancy as such but rather a theology of both complete devotion and growth. The infant is the ideal sacramental subject not because of his innocence or inner life but because he does each activity with undivided attention. An infant comes to the sacraments in the same manner as he sucks at his mother's breast. At that particular moment nothing else in the whole world matters. The image remains the ideal for Christian growth. The adult who eats the eucharist and becomes an infant inwardly[1] is at that moment completely given over to God. It is in this light that we must seriously re-examine our common assumption that age has something to do with Christian maturity. It is as a corollary to that question that the question of an infant's capability to receive the eucharist is resolved.

The final question implicit in the communion of the very young is one which churches are posing in a fresh way today. It is that of community. If the International Year of the Child brought one thing to public attention it was perhaps the unique status of children in society. We have tended in the past to treat children as diminutive adults with no real contribution to make to society until they are adult. Slowly we are becoming aware of the qualities reflected in children's lives that reflect forgotten, yet important, aspects of our own lives. These are qualities that transcend the social barriers of not only sex and race and class, but also the barriers of language and time. The inclusion of these qualities in our worship is imperative if we are to have worship that is truly catholic.

The passing of Christendom has made parishes and whole churches examine Christian community anew. They can no longer expect society as a whole to nourish the young in Christian values nor can they expect

[1] Augustine *Tract. in Joh.* XXVI, 1.

that same society to support those who are still young in Christ. Society is apathetic if not hostile to Christian values and the Gospel. In such an environment the reliance of the Church on the societal nurture of its young is no longer possible. Christian communities become smaller, and they must take upon themselves the responsibility for helping their young to grow in Christ and in faith.

This societal change has profoundly affected the church's conception of community. The Christian community can no longer be equated with society as a whole but rather with the extended family that meets regularly around the Lord's Table. Children take on a new role in that community. They are no longer assumed as simply a part of the biological fact, but rather become a sign of the continuance of something that is much less sure than it once was. The question of including those members of the community in the fellowship of the Table becomes a real one. The image of the family for the Christian community and the family meal for the parish eucharist, both of which have become so common in the past decade, force the issue at the pastoral level.

The rest must be left to experience. It is difficult to articulate the profound effect the admission of the very young has had on the community life of parishes. Some lay people speak of it in terms of conversion. They know they cannot go back to their old ways. In making the Lord's Table the place where young and old, rich and poor, all share a common meal they suddenly realize something new and profound about the nature of the community to which Christ calls them. Children who have received the eucharist from an early age and have grown to reflect on that experience often do so in terms of profound spiritual insight. For them it has signified the existence of a society in which they too have gifts to offer and in which their importance is equal to that of the adults—a place where they feel they belong and where they want to stay.

I became most acutely aware of all this when leaving my parish in Canada to continue with my academic work. When the lay people of the parish were meeting with the Archbishop to discuss their new priest they were asked what they wanted the new priest to do. Of the many things they might have asked for—and it was a parish that might best have asked for an organizer or a money-raiser—their two requests were for a priest who would celebrate the eucharist with them each week and who would continue to give communion to the infants and young children who came to that eucharist.

APPENDIX 1 PROGRESS IN THE ANGLICAN COMMUNION

I attempted to make a general survey of the available literature in an article in *Studia Liturgica* XXI, 2-3 (1977) p.129ff.

Pushed by the Lambeth Conference of 1958 'to explore the theology of baptism and confirmation in relation to the need to commission the laity for their task in the world, and to experiment in this regard' (Lambeth 1968, *Resolutions and Reports,* p.37), a number of Anglican provinces set their doctrinal commissions to work on the question of Christian Initiation.

Working independently the various commissions came to conclusions that are typified by that of the Doctrinal Commission of the Church in Wales:

'Any separation of [Christian Initiation as: participation in the death and resurrection of Christ; New Birth from above; gifting of the Holy Spirit; and admission to Holy Communion] *either* as successively given at different stages in the initiation rite, *or* as conceivable in isolation from one another, involves grave theological confusion. This is why the disintegrated pattern of Initiation, which the Western Church has inherited, is theologically unsatisfactory. Such separation leads to pseudo-problems that are insoluble theologically, if not in fact meaningless.' (*Christian Initiation,* 1971, p.22).

Acting on conclusions of this sort liturgical commissions prepared a variety of rites with an underlying rationale that can be expressed in the words of the American Liturgical Commission:

'1. There is one, and only one, unrepeatable act of Christian initiation which makes a person a member of the Body of Christ.

2. The essential element of Christian initiation is baptism by water and the Spirit, in the Name of the Holy Trinity, in response to repentance and faith.

3. Christian initiation is normatively administered in a liturgical rite that also includes the laying on of hands, consignation (with or without Chrism), prayer for the gift of the Holy Spirit, reception by the Christian Community, joining the eucharistic fellowship, and commissioning for the Christian mission. When a bishop is present, it is expected that he will preside at the rite.' (*Prayer Book Studies* 29, p.64).

These rites met a variety of reaction when they met their respective national synods. In some they were welcomed and accepted as presented. In many more they met the stumbling block of Confirmation. Many bishops defined much of their pastoral ministry in terms of their confirmation visitations, and delegates were unwilling to lose what they saw as a rite of passage to Christian maturity. (For a discussion of the problems of confirmation as it is faced by the churches at large see my article 'Confirmation in the 1980's' in the WCC commentary on the document *One Baptism . . .*). The general result of these synodical debates was to insist that a rite be provided for the mature affirmation of baptismal vows (confirmation in the reformed sense).

Where provinces accepted the proposals (with the provision of a later affirmation rite) the pattern has become baptism with laying on of hands/chrismation, communion either at baptism or an early age, affirmation (at an older age than has been customary for confirmation).

Over the five to ten years that this pattern has been in effect there have been several observable phenomena. Minimum age limits for communicants, where established (Canada, New Zealand), have been eliminated. The average age of communicants has fallen steadily (parents, and particularly children, could not see why a five-year-old could communicate while his three-year-old sibling could not). The baptismal communion of infants is no longer a novelty.

Baptismal discipline as a whole has become more rigorous. Parish priests are less willing to baptize on demand. Initiation is a public event in the context of the Sunday morning liturgy and tends to be associated with major festivals (Easter, Pentecost, Christmas, Baptism of Christ/Epiphany) rather than being determined by granny's visit from overseas. Parents are taking the whole matter more seriously. Baptism is less and less a social rite but, when faced with the new pattern, particularly the question of the baptismal eucharist, it is becoming a moment when families decide just where they stand in relation to the Gospel and the Church, often deciding not to have their infant baptized because they are not prepared to make the commitment the Church asks of them.

APPENDIX 2 INFANT AND CHILD COMMUNION IN THE CHURCH OF ENGLAND

by Colin Buchanan

David Holeton's Study arises from his experience in Canada and the United States, which in turn led to his further historical researches. It is a very timely contribution to a situation in the Church of England which has seemed much more stuck, though the theological imperative for admitting the baptized to communion with their parents *ab initio* is no less. The purpose of this somewhat more journalistic appendix is to report to the large majority of readers who are English Anglicans what their own situation is, and to inform other readers in other parts of the world about it also.

Pressure for child communion must have been there, even if somewhat inarticulately, from the early days of the Parish Communion. I have endeavoured to trace the origins of the 'blessing of children at the communion rail', which obviously grew with the practice of whole families coming forward to the rail together—or in some place whole Sunday School classes, or other groupings being incorporated into the Parish Communion. I have not so far unearthed any claims to have originated the practice, but my guess is that it began in the late forties, though possibly in the thirties. It is typical of Anglicanism that this now staple feature of the Parish Communion has never received any rubrical or other recognition in all the years of its practice. It simply goes on—and has spread through the world. Its highly anomalous character advertises its interim nature—it must surely have been introduced as a halfway step to giving communion, and have been deliberately designed to be unsatisfactory in order to lead the church on towards the real goal? In the event it remains with us, without rubric, without text (I tried to find out in *News of Liturgy* a few years ago what texts were in use *de facto,* with very odd results), and without rationale. Young children ask for the bread and the cup, and are given if not a stone at least an unwarranted substitute. Parents who do not think their children should be excluded find themselves groping around for reasons to give to their own believing children why they are in fact denied the sacarament.

There was a slowly rising groundswell on this issue in the Church of England in the 1950s and 1960s—a groundswell obviously led by the Parish Communion participants, but not wholly confined to them. Indeed the National Evangelical Anglican Congress at Keele in 1967, whilst it called for communion to be central to the Church's worship (thus indicating strongly that it was not in fact so already among the participants)[1], also included in its statement:

> 'We call for further theological study as to whether the age of discretion is always the right time for admission to Holy

[1] Philip Crowe (ed.) *Keele '67* (Falcon, London, 1967).

Communion. Some of us would like the children of Christian families to be admitted as communicants at an early age . . .'[1]

This came from the part of the Church of England where it might have been least expected. It is one indication that the tide was already running in the late 1960s.[2]

In Autumn 1969 the 'Ely' Commission was appointed to look at questions of Christian initiation, and the Commission presented its report in Spring 1971.[3] The relevant part of their recommendations ran as follows:

'Concerning admission to Communion, we recommend that:

1. *It be permissible for the parish priest at his discretion, to admit persons to Communion (if they so desire) who have been baptized with water in the name of the Trinity.*

2. *Adequate preparation for admission to Communion be provided and be such as to enable the candidates to participate fully in the Eucharist.*

3. *The first Communion be administered, wherever possible, by the bishop.'*[4]

It looks as though the Commission members had in mind an age of admission of around seven or eight years of age, and the concept of preparation by the church, and the running of a 'class' who then all came to 'first Communion' at the same time (for that would be necessary in order to have the bishop presiding). This could by no stretch of the imagination be viewed as ushering in *infant* communion though it was clearly a first step in that direction. The theological framework within which this was to fit included:

1. An insistence that baptism alone was complete sacramental initiation which therefore in principle qualified the recipients for communion.

2. A recommendation that what was previously known as 'confirmation' should be delayed until, e.g., sixteen years of age, and should represent a responsible commitment to adult Christian discipleship.

---

[1] *ibid.* paragraph 74, p.35. A similar statement appears in the findings of the second National Evangelical Anglican Congress in 1977: 'We are divided on the advisability of admitting children to Communion. Some . . . Others advocate a variation of the traditional order and the admission to Holy Communion of baptized children of communicant parents after due preparation . . .' (*The Nottingham Statement* (Falcon, London, 1977) paragraph G4, pp.28-9). This statement was however the findings of a group, not those of the whole Congress. It does start to open the question, not tackled here, of whether any discrimination is to be practised as to which children should be admitted to communion.

[2] Thus, to take a different sort of instance, the pre-synodical London Diocesan Conference passed a resolution desiring that baptized children should be admissible to communion during 1969.

[3] *Christian Initiation: Birth and Growth in the Christian Society* (Church Information Office,, London, 1971).

[4] *Id* paragraph 121, p.42.

The Commission was obviously fearful that the existing bishops of the Church of England would worry lest confirmation be downgraded, and lest their own pastoral role in confirmation be correspondingly diminished, so there was much use of phrases like 'an enhanced role for the bishop'. It may have been this concern which led to the inclusion of the bishop's presidency at 'first communion' in their recommendations about admission to communion—a tactical move in order to assist the promotion of the main change.

The General Synod had a first canter over the ground in July 1971, but then did not return to the report until February 1974. Then the Synod passed the following motion:

'That this Synod, recognizing that there are divergent theological understandings of Christian Initiation held within the Church:
(i) accepts the principle that full sacramental participation within the Church may precede a mature Profession of Faith;
(ii) invites the Standing Committee to ask the dioceses if they would support a reordering of initiation practice according to this principle by one or more of the following means within a continuing framework of training for the Christian life:
(a) admission of baptized persons to the Holy Communion at the discretion of the parish priest in consultation with the Bishop followed by Confirmation at the hands of the Bishop;
(b) uniting the laying on of hands and/or anointing with oil to Baptism, followed after due preparation by admission to Holy Communion at the discretion of the parish priest: and subsequently providing an opportunity, where appropriate, for a solemn affirmation of baptismal promises accompanied by a further laying on of hands;
and to report their views to the Secretary-General by January 1976.'[1]

This package of questions was then sent to the dioceses.

The diocesan returns were very equivocal. Only 20 out of 38 diocesan synods which sent in countable returns favoured the principle of earlier admission to communion, and in separate voting on (a) and (b) above the former was lost in 22 dioceses out of 36 and the latter in 32 out of 36.[2]

It may be possible to read a little deeper into the significance of the diocesan voting. It is of course odd that a diocese should accept the principle, but turn down both alternative methods of implementing it (which evidently happened in a few cases)—but it is clear that if the supporters of the principle divided into half for and half against each of the alternatives presented, then the half against, when joined with the minority opposed to the whole principle, might become a majority. And

1 This and other synodical material quoted can be traced in the appropriate part of the Synod's *Report of Proceedings*.
2 *Christian Initiation: Results of the Reference to The Diocesan Synods: 1974-75* (GS 291A) (Church Information Office, London, 1976).

this happened. Furthermore, voting was by houses, and any one house could defeat a motion—even the bishop on his own being one such house.

More important is the fact that a large number of members of the Church of England could still not focus the question of principle. In parishes which do not have a Parish Communion weekly, the children are rarely , if ever, present at a communion service, and the oddity and absurdity of their being refused communion does not emerge. Indeed the evangelical wing of the Church of England has tended to want instruction at a relatively mature age, and a cerebral grasp of Christian truth, before admission to communion, and the confirmation classes have been the guarantees employed that this is given. Thus on one wing of the church were persons ready to vote against the principle, and in the voting they combined, it would seem, with those who either feared to accept the principle lest they then get landed with what looked like the wrong implementation of the principle[1], or, having voted for the principle then divided over its implementation. It was a slightly sorry mess.

Thus when the issue came back before General Synod in July 1976, the Standing Committee warned the members that there would be great difficulties in implementing the principle in view of the divided condition of the Church. The motion they tabled, not as their own recommendation, but to enable the Synod to find its mind, ran as follows:

'That this Synod, accepting that full sacramental participation within the Church may precede a mature Profession of Faith, supports the proposition that alternative provision should be made for the ordering of initiation practice within the Church of England, provided that any revised order is set within a continuing framework of training for the Christian life.'

However, the Synod, dampened by the diocesan returns, voted against this motion as follows:

	Ayes	Noes
Bishops	17	27
Clergy	83	132
Laity	86	112

Finally, when the issue seemed to have come to this dead stop, the Synod passed a motion by the Bishop of Newcastle (since then translated to Southwark):

'That Diocesan Bishops, in consultation with their Synods, be invited to make wider use of the discretion already allowed by Canon B.27, so as to admit young children to Confirmation when so requested; and to take steps to encourage the periodic renewal of baptismal vows in adult life, especially by those who have been baptized and confirmed in childhood.'

[1] In particular this has reference to those 'two-stage' sacramentalists, who, whatever they thought about children participating in the eucharist on principle, were wholly opposed to any anticipating of confirmation in order to achieve this result.

This would seem to stretch the age of confirmation down a bit lower, so as to admit, say, eight-year-olds to confirmation and communion in occasional circumstances. But it is extremely doubtful whether Canon B.27 does in fact give any such discretion, and there is little evidence to hand that diocesan bishops have, in the five years since this motion was passed, actually consulted their diocesan synods on the issue.

None of this, however, means that the issue is dead. When the Ely report first came out, even before Synod passed its motion of February 1974, the then Bishop of Southwark declared some deaneries in his diocese to be areas of experiment, where young children would be admitted to communion long prior to confirmation. Naturally, once started, this practice continues to the present day. Similarly, the diocese of Manchester has had a most detailed survey of the theological issue made by a special commission, and the commission's findings would involve a similar change of practice. In my own diocese, Southwell, the bishop has encouraged a controlled experiment of the same sort.[1] And at the time of writing there has come onto the General Synod agenda a diocesan motion from Winchester—a motion reflecting the response of that diocese to the original reference to the dioceses in 1974-6, and also reflecting the mood of that diocese to-day:

'That this Synod

(a) confirms its resolution passed in November 1975 and supports the proposed admission of baptized persons to the Holy Communion at the discretion of the parish priest in consultation with the bishop, followed at a later stage by confirmation, subject to the adoption by the incumbent, the parish and the family concerned of guidelines approved by this Synod;

(b) requests the General Synod to review its resolution of July 1976 disallowing the admission of baptized persons to the Holy Communion followed at a later stage by Confirmation; and in the light of the growing demand for such an option, urges the General Synod to permit the introduction of this change in certain dioceses for a period of twelve years as a pilot experiment.'

This motion has yet to be debated in General Synod, but its appearance on the agenda gives hope that the Church of England may yet take steps to join its sister-Churches in Canada, the United States, New Zealand, and elsewhere[2] in affirming that child communion is the proper concomitant of infant baptism.

---

[1] It is this parish, St. Peter's and St. Paul's Hucknall, which is portrayed to illustrate the same principle in Colin Buchanan, Trevor Lloyd, Harold Miller (eds.) *Anglican Worship Today: Collins' Illustrated Guide to the Alternative Service Book* (Collins Liturgical Publications, London, 1980) p.160.

[2] The first steps toward this have just been taken in Australia. There is also evidence of non-Anglican Churches moving in the same direction in some parts of the world.